Overcoming

emotional breakdown

By

Lucy Becker

TABLE OF CONTENTS

Introduction

The first step is to comprehend how unpleasant emotions and feelings function. Then, we must learn how to rewire those feelings and reverse them. If you take the suggested actions, you can live a happier life. It's human nature to want to love, be loved, and feel appreciated. It appears simple enough, yet for the majority of people, it is a daily, often silent fight. You lose energy, feel downhearted, and become stuck when you are experiencing toxic emotions like fear, resentment, guilt, and shame. Without careful attention and healing, it's simple to fall victim to faulty thinking patterns that create negative emotional and energy "imprints." Our experiences and responses to the world are shaped by these imprints. It can be difficult and challenging to go through emotional breakdowns. *An emotional breakdown is a condition of severe emotional anguish that can be brought on by a number of stressors, including traumatic events, interpersonal problems, financial difficulty, or work-related stress.*

When someone has an emotional breakdown, they could feel helpless, overwhelmed, and unable to control their feelings. Also, they might feel physical symptoms like chest pain, a fast heartbeat, or trouble breathing. *It's critical to realize that everyone is susceptible to emotional breakdowns, which are a common reaction to stress. The person's* physical and mental health may suffer if they are not treated, though. It's crucial to get treatment if you or someone you love is going through a mental breakdown. This may entail getting professional help, consulting a friend or relative you may trust, or calling a crisis hotline. It's also crucial to refrain from taking drugs or alcohol to deal with your emotions because doing so could make things worse. In general, it's crucial to be aware of the warning signals of an emotional breakdown and to act to get support and take care of oneself. In the face of stress and challenging emotions, it is possible to bounce back and develop resilience by doing this.

getting over your negative emotions
Although overcoming poisonous emotions can be a difficult process, it is unquestionably possible with persistent effort and determination. The first step is to

identify and label the feelings that are upsetting you. Are you feeling dread, guilt, shame, guilt, or rage? You can begin to address the feelings once you have identified them. Negative attitudes and thoughts frequently act as fuel for toxic emotions. Challenge those ideas and try to replace them with ones that are more uplifting and grounded in reality. Try thinking, for instance, "I've made mistakes, but I'm still learning and growing" rather than "I'm a failure." Treating yourself with kindness and empathy in the same way that you would a friend will go a long way. *This entails accepting your feelings and experiences without condemnation or judgment. You can become more conscious of your thoughts and feelings by practicing mindfulness meditation, which will enable you to remain objective about them.* You may be able to manage your emotions and acquire more perspective as a result. It's good to take things slowly and keep in mind that eradicating poisonous emotions is a process. Be kind to yourself and persevere in your quest for emotional growth and healing. Any emotion that surfaces during an emotional breakdown is OK, including feelings of overwhelm, sadness, anger, and others. Without passing judgment, permit yourself to feel what you are feeling. Even when you're depressed, it's crucial to allow yourself to experience your emotions. The human experience includes emotions naturally, and attempting to ignore or conceal them might actually make them stronger and more difficult to manage. Instead, make an effort to impartially acknowledge and accept your emotions. Give yourself time and space to process your feelings of sadness, rage, frustration, or anything else you may be going through. Writing in a journal, speaking with a close friend or therapist, or engaging in self-care practices like taking a bath or going for a walk could all prove to be beneficial. Keep in mind that sometimes feeling bad is okay. Everyone experiences challenging moments, so it's crucial to practice self-compassion and gentleness when you're going through them. You may start to heal and move forward in a healthy way by allowing yourself permission to express your feelings.

Chapter 1

Learning about emotional problems

**Specific emotional collapses*

Based on their underlying causes and symptoms, emotional breakdowns can be generally divided into many categories.

When a person faces ongoing stress from their jobs, studies, or personal lives, they can experience burnout, a sort of emotional breakdown. It can result in fatigue, disconnection, and a sense of being overpowered.

panic attacks acute bout of fear and anxiety known as a can be brought on by a variety of stressors, including traumatic events, phobias, or social settings. Breathing difficulties, perspiration, chest pain, and a fluttering heart are among symptoms that can occur.

Depression is a mood condition marked by feelings of melancholy, hopelessness, and a loss of interest in once-pleasurable activities. Genetics, pressures from the environment, gathering and chemical imbalances in the brain are just a few of the potential causes.

Anxiety: Anxiety is a disorder that is characterized by excessive concern and anxiety, frequently in relation to certain circumstances or things. Physical signs including perspiration, heart palpitations, and trembling may result from it.

***Post-traumatic stress disorder
(PTSD)*** is a mental health issue
that can arise after going through
or witnessing a stressful incident,
such as a fight, an assault, or a
natural disaster. Nightmares,
flashbacks, and avoidance
behaviors are a few symptoms that
may appear.

personality disorder (BPD) isThe
mental illness known as
borderline characterized by

impulsive behaviors, intense and unstable emotions, and a skewed sense of self. It might result in a tendency to engage in self-destructive behaviors, feelings of emptiness, and a dread of abandonment.

bipolar disorder is a period of intense highs (mania) and lows (depression) are symptoms of a mood condition (depression). Extreme mood swings, sleep issues, and problems focusing can all result from it.

Emotional breakdown signs and symptoms

Depending on the person and the underlying causes, emotional breakdowns can show themselves in various ways and have distinct symptoms.

very depressing or hopeless emotions that persist.

*feelings of worthlessness, hopelessness, or assistance.

*excessive concern or stress that disrupts daily activity.

*difficulty focusing or making choices.

*a decline in interest in formerly enjoyable activities.

*withdrawal from interpersonal interactions and social settings.

*sleep patterns that have changed due to sleeplessness or oversleeping.

*modifications to appetite or weight.

*physical signs such headaches, stomachaches, or exhaustion.

*irritability, hostility, or mood changes.

*Suicidal or self-destructive thoughts.

*preventing emotional collapse and resentment

reasons for emotional instability

Several things can lead to emotional breakdowns. Excessive amounts of stress brought on by work, relationships, money concerns, or health problems can all lead to emotional breakdowns

Trauma: Emotional breakdowns can be brought on by past trauma, such as abuse or a substantial loss.

Mental illness: Those who suffer from depression, anxiety, or other mental illnesses may be more prone to emotional breakdowns.

Abuse of drugs or alcohol can interfere with the brain's capacity to control emotions and increase the likelihood of emotional breakdowns.

Absence of support: Emotional breakdowns can also be brought on by feeling alone or unsupported.

Physical exhaustion: Emotional instability and breakdowns can be caused by prolonged fatigue or a lack of sleep.

Major life changes: Major life events such as a divorce, moving to a new city, or losing a job can also trigger emotional breakdowns.

Emotional resentment's root causes

Instances of perceived wrongdoing by an individual can give rise to resentment, and these instances are frequently initiated by complaints of unfairness or humiliation. The sense of being the target of ongoing discrimination or prejudice, feeling envious of others, feeling used or taken advantage of, and having accomplishments go unnoticed while others flourish without putting in as much effort are all common causes of resentment. Moreover, dyadic interactions such as emotional rejection or denial by another person, purposeful embarrassment or belittling by another person, or ignorance, putting down, or derision by another person can all result in a generation of resentment. By repeatedly dwelling on old complaints, such as distressing memories of painful experiences, or by making excuses for the feeling, resentment can also grow and be perpetuated. Therefore, the grieving process can lead to resentment, which can then be maintained by ruminating. Looking for symptoms like the need for emotion control, acting happy around someone to mask genuine feelings toward them, or using sarcastic or insulting language while speaking to or about them can all be used to self-diagnose resentment. It can also be identified by the emergence of agitation- or depression-related emotions, such as feeling down or hopeless for no apparent reason, getting furious without cause, *or experiencing nightmares or unsettling daydreams about a certain individual.*

Chapter 2

The effects of emotional breakdowns

How disruptions in emotion can impact our life, Breakdowns on the emotional, mental, or emotional levels can have a big impact on our life. When someone is unable to handle daily life due to overwhelming emotions like despair, worry, rage, or stress, they are said to have experienced an emotional breakdown.

Physical health: Physical health issues including headaches, lethargy, stomachaches, and insomnia can result from emotional breakdowns. The body's response to prolonged stress can also increase the likelihood of acquiring chronic health disorders, such as cardiovascular disease and diabetes.

Mental health: Subsequent mental health disorders like sadness or anxiety can show themselves as emotional breakdowns. These illnesses can get worse and affect every aspect of a person's life if they are not treated.

Relationships:
Emotional breakdowns can cause tension in bonds with friends, family, and coworkers. Conflict and social isolation might result from others' inability to cope with the strong emotions and behaviors linked to breakdowns.

Work and productivity: Emotional breakdowns can affect a person's capacity for daily activities, concentration, and decision-making. Reduced productivity, absenteeism, and even job loss may result from this.

quality and aspect of lives

Emotional breakdowns can drastically lower a person's general quality of life. They could find it challenging to enjoy the things they once found enjoyable.

Chapter 3

How emotional breakdowns affect our physical and mental wellbeing

Our mental and physical health can be significantly impacted by emotional breakdowns. They are frequently accompanied by strong emotions of melancholy, anxiety, helplessness, and weariness that can be debilitating and difficult to control.

Impacts on mental health:

Depression and anxiety disorders are more likely to develop in those who experience emotional breakdowns.

Having a lower sense of self-worth and confidence can cause feelings of inadequacy and self-doubt in those who have gone through emotional breakdowns.

Concentration problems: Emotional breakdowns can make it difficult for a person to concentrate and focus on duties, which lowers productivity and performance in school or the workplace.

Relationship strain: Because of the intensity and unpredictability of the emotions involved, emotional breakdowns can strain relationships with friends, family, and coworkers.

Impacts on Physical Health

Emotional breakdowns can interfere with normal sleep cycles and make it difficult to go sleep, stay asleep, or have restorative sleep.

Fatigue and exhaustion: Individuals who are having emotional breakdowns may feel drained and lack energy, making it difficult for them to go about their everyday lives.

gastrointestinal issues: Stress and worry brought on by emotional breakdowns can result in gastrointestinal issues like nausea, diarrhea, and stomach pain.

Cardiovascular issues: Long-term stress resulting from emotional breakdowns raises the risk of cardiovascular issues such as high blood pressure, heart disease, and stroke.

Emotional breakdowns'

effects on our relationships

Relationships can be significantly impacted by emotional breakdowns in both positive and negative ways. Emotional breakdowns can also leave us more exposed and susceptible to other influences. While in some circumstances this can be advantageous, it can also leave us vulnerable to being injured or manipulated by others who prey on our weaknesses.

Communication challenges
Emotional breakdowns might hinder our ability to communicate clearly with others. We might find it difficult to communicate our ideas and emotions clearly, which can result in misunderstandings and poor communication.

Relationship Tension: When we are experiencing emotional distress, we may become more irritable or easily upset, which can cause relationship tension. Our connections with others may be strained by this tension, which can also make it more difficult to preserve healthy relationships.

Increased Empathy: On the other hand, experiencing an emotional breakdown can also make you more understanding and empathetic toward other people. When we are experiencing a tough moment, we may be more sensitive to the needs and feelings of those around us, resulting in stronger connections and more meaningful relationships.

Greater intimacy

Emotional breakdowns may lead to an increase in the level of intimacy in our relationships. We could discover that we can build stronger emotional connections with individuals around us when we permit ourselves to be vulnerable. In general, emotional breakdowns can have a complicated web of impacts on our interpersonal connections. Although managing our emotions can be difficult, we can learn to do it in a way that enhances rather than erodes our relationships with others with time and effort.

Chapter 4

Avoiding Emotional Breakdowns

1. Determine the reason

Attempt to identify what caused your emotional collapse. Is it connected to a specific incident or circumstance? Addressing the root cause can be made easier with an understanding of the problem. Recognize and accept your feelings: Even if they seem overwhelming, it's critical to recognize and embrace your feelings. You can then begin the process of determining what caused your emotional collapse. Retrace your steps. If you can, try to get away from the circumstance that led to your emotional collapse. Inhale deeply a few times as you attempt to relax.

Consider for a moment what might have caused your emotional breakdown. Consider any recent occurrences or circumstances that might have influenced your mental state. Contact someone. Think about sharing your feelings with someone you can trust. *They might be able to support you and assist you in determining what caused your emotional breakdown.* Consider obtaining professional assistance from a therapist or counselor if you're having problems determining the reason for your emotional breakdown. They can assist you in examining your emotions and locating any underlying problems that can be influencing your emotional condition.

2. Ask for assistance

Discuss your situation with a trusted friend or relative. It might be a friend, relative, or therapy. An emotional breakdown can be fought off with the support of a friend or family member. Reaching out for assistance is a terrific first step when it comes to taking care of oneself during difficult times. To your requirements and preferences, a variety of options are available for emotional assistance. Sometimes, just talking to someone concerned about you and who will listen to you without passing judgment can be beneficial. Contact an expert in mental health. A therapist or counselor can offer a private, safe setting for discussing current issues and formulating coping mechanisms. A therapist or counselor can offer a private, secure setting where you can discuss your issues and create coping mechanisms. You can use online directories to look for therapists in your region or ask your doctor for a recommendation. Keep in mind that asking for assistance when you need it is acceptable. You don't need to experience this alone.

3. *Look after your physical well-being*

By getting adequate sleep, eating well, and exercising, you can take good care of your body. These routines can help you feel happier and less stressed. Given the connection between the two, it's crucial to look after your physical health while you're feeling low. It can be tempting to overlook your physical health while you're experiencing emotional lows, but caring for your body can help elevate your spirits and improve your mood. A little walk or some light stretching will help release endorphins and lift your spirits. Consume a healthy diet. Eat as much fruit, veggies, lean protein, and complete grains as you can. Avoid processed or sugary foods because they can affect mood. Sleep enough, Set a regular sleep routine, and try to get 7-8 hours of sleep each night. Do not use drugs or alcohol. Although it may be tempting to use drinks or drugs as a coping mechanism for challenging emotions, doing so might worsen your mood over time. Put relaxation techniques to use: Yoga, meditation, and deep breathing exercises can all help you feel better and reduce stress. Keep in mind that looking after your physical health is a crucial aspect of self-care and can improve your mood on both a mental and physical level. Never be afraid to ask a mental health expert for help if you are having emotional problems.

4. *Engage in self-care*

Take part in enjoyable activities, such as reading a book or watching a movie. Spend some time doing something you want to do to unwind. To feel better when you're emotionally low, it's crucial to look for yourself. Be always patient and compassionate to yourself. Recognize and believe that everyone experiences difficult moments and that it's okay to feel the way you do. Spending time with loved ones and participating in social activities, on the other hand, can be advantageous. You can maintain your composure and grounding by engaging in mindfulness techniques like meditation and deep breathing. Keep in mind that self-care is a continuous process, therefore it's crucial to give it a priority in your life. Taking care of oneself will help you develop mentally and emotionally.

Chapter 5

Taking Action

Have a worry-free existence by overcoming negative mind patterns.

Although negative thought patterns can be challenging to break and can depress you emotionally, it is possible to live a worry-free life by using specific strategies and practices.

Recognize your negative mental processes. Recognizing your negative thought patterns is the first step. Observe when and why you get negative ideas. If you're aware of them, you may start to challenge them and swap out negative thoughts for constructive ones. Gratitude can also assist you in changing your attention from negative to positive thoughts. Spend some time every day thinking about your blessings, no matter how minor. Employy uplifting statements, Repeat to yourself encouraging statements like "I am capable" or "I am worthy." By doing this, you can rewire your subconscious mind and start talking to yourself positively instead of negatively. Dispute unfavorable perceptions, When unfavorable notions come to mind, disprove them with facts. For instance, if you are concerned that you will fail at a task, consider times when you have succeeded in comparable projects.

Read uplifting books, listen to uplifting music, and be among positive people. You may be able to keep an optimistic mindset and lessen your negative thought patterns as a result. Consider seeking out professional assistance from a therapist or counselor if your negative thought patterns are significantly distressing you or interfering with your everyday life. Keep in mind that changing unhelpful mental habits requires time and effort.

Be kind to yourself and acknowledge minor accomplishments along the way. You can develop the ability to live a worry-free life with practice.

Creating a fulfilling existence

Intentional activities and a positive outlook are necessary to manifest a more lively and satisfying life. Imagine the life you want to lead, Think of your ideal existence while closing your eyes. How would it appear? Which action would you take? Would you be somewhere? Who would be in your immediate vicinity? The greater your visualization, the more vivid and specific it should be. Set definite, specific goals based on your visualization to help you live your perfect life. Set deadlines for each phase of your goals by breaking them down into smaller, more doable chunks. Recognize your ability to fulfill your dreams and achieve your goals. Avoid negative self-talk and self-doubt. Instead, concentrate on your abilities and achievements. No matter how little the steps, make progress toward your goals every day. The secret to creating the life you want is to consistently take action. Remain upbeat. Focus on the positive aspects of your life and surround yourself with happiness. Try to be mindful and grateful, and refrain from concentrating on anything unpleasant. Accept change, You might need to push yourself beyond your comfort zone and make changes to manifest a more lively existence. Accept change and be receptive to fresh encounters and chances. Make time for enjoyable and relaxing pursuits like exercise, meditation, and time spent in nature. Always keep in mind that creating a more fulfilling and colorful existence is a process that may require time and effort. Hold fast to your objectives and have faith in the process.

Chapter 6:

Handling Emotional Breakdowns

The management of emotional breakdowns can benefit greatly from therapy. Those who go through emotional breakdowns may feel overburdened, nervous, or sad, and they may find it difficult to deal with their emotions. Individuals can explore and process their feelings in a safe and encouraging setting during therapy. One of the key benefits of therapy is that it can help individuals acquire coping skills and techniques to regulate their emotions more effectively

To help people manage their emotions and lessen stress, therapists might impart skills like mindfulness, relaxation, and ***cognitive-behavioral therapy (CBT).*** A place for people to express and process their feelings can be offered through therapy. Individuals can better understand their emotions and the root causes of their emotional breakdowns by speaking with a skilled specialist about them. This can help people become more self-aware and enable them to recognize and deal with any unfavorthoughtsughts or behavioral habits. Moreover, therapy can provide people with the emotional support and affirmation they need to deal with emotional breakdowns. Therapy can be a useful tool in controlling emotional breakdowns because a therapist can offer a sympathetic, nonjudgmental ear to hear about people's experiences and provide advice and support while they work through their feelings. Therapy can help people better manage their emotions and lead more fulfilled lives by offering coping strategies, emotional support, and a secure space for them to explore their feelings.

In Conclusion

Your mental and physical health will suffer if you experience emotional breakdowns. These feelings encompass dread, remorse, humiliation, resentment, envy, *and jealousy.* If these emotions aren't dealt with, they can result in tension and worry, which can then lead to depression, physical sickness, and chronic pain. It might be challenging to feel joyful, satisfied, or at peace while you are dealing with poisonous emotions. Conflicts brought on by toxic emotions might make it difficult to establish good connections with others. lowering your self-confidence, It might lower your self-esteem and cause you to question your skills if you are overtaken by poisonous emotions. Damaging your well-being, Prolonged emotional trauma can result in physical health difficulties like high blood pressure, heart disease, and digestive disorders. Identifying the precise feelings that are upsetting you and working on coping mechanisms will help you overcome toxic emotions and boost your happiness. *This can entail learning constructive coping skills, getting help from a therapist or counselor, or engaging in relaxation and mindfulness exercises.*

If your emotional breakdown is serious and interfering with your daily life, think about getting professional treatment from a therapist or mental health expert. Keep in mind that having emotional breakdowns is normal. You may overcome these difficulties and proceed by taking care of yourself and getting support.